Gluten Free Cookbook

© Copyright 2021 - All rights reserved.

You may not reproduce, duplicate or send the contents of this book without direct written permission from the author. You cannot hereby despite any circumstance blame the publisher or hold him or her to legal responsibility for any reparation, compensations, or monetary forfeiture owing to the information included herein, either in a direct or an indirect way.

Legal Notice: This book has copyright protection. You can use the book for personal purpose. You should not sell, use, alter, distribute, quote, take excerpts or paraphrase in part or whole the material contained in this book without obtaining the permission of the author first.

Disclaimer Notice: You must take note that the information in this document is for casual reading and entertainment purposes only.
We have made every attempt to provide accurate, up to date and reliable information. We do not express or imply guarantees of any kind. The persons who read admit that the writer is not occupied in giving legal, financial, medical or other advice. We put this book content by sourcing various places.

Please consult a licensed professional before you try any techniques shown in this book. By going through this document, the book lover comes to an agreement that under no situation is the author accountable for any forfeiture, direct or indirect, which they may incur because of the use of material contained in this document, including, but not limited to, — errors, omissions, or inaccuracies.

Whether it's delicious vegetarian or vegan recipes you're after, or ideas for gluten - free dishes, you'll find plenty here to inspire you.

Enjoy this tested collection of gluten free recipes. Whether breakfast, dessert or baking, these easy recipes will add excitement to your meals!

Chicken paillards with radicchio slaw (gluten-free)

INGREDIENTS

1 radicchio, finely shredded
4 celery stalks, thinly sliced
2 Granny Smith apples, cut into matchsticks
1 cup basil leaves, shredded
1/2 cup walnuts, toasted
1/4 cup (60ml) balsamic vinegar
1/2 cup (125ml) extra virgin olive oil, plus 1 tablespoon to cook chicken
1 teaspoon Dijon mustard
2 chicken breast fillets
20g unsalted butter
Lemon wedges, to serve

METHOD

1. Place the radicchio, celery, apple, basil and walnuts in a bowl. In a separate bowl, whisk together the vinegar, oil and mustard. Season to taste, then toss with the salad ingredients and set aside.
2. Cut each chicken breast through the centre into 2 thin fillets. Place each fillet between 2 pieces of plastic wrap and pound with a meat mallet or rolling pin until thin. Season with salt and pepper.
3. Melt the butter with the extra tablespoon of oil in a large frypan over high heat. Add the chicken and cook for 2 minutes on each side or until golden and cooked through.
4. Divide the chicken and salad among 4 plates and serve with lemon wedges.

Pancetta and cannellini bean risotto (gluten-free)

INGREDIENTS
- 1 tbs olive oil
- 100g sliced pancetta
- 1/2 tsp fennel seeds
- 50g unsalted butter
- 1 onion, finely chopped
- 1 garlic clove, finely chopped
- 2 tsp finely chopped rosemary
- 8 thyme sprigs, leaves picked, plus extra leaves to serve
- 1 1/2 cups (330g) arborio rice
- 1/3 cup (80ml) dry white wine
- 1.5L (6 cups) gluten-free chicken stock, heated
- 400g can cannellini beans, rinsed, drained
- 1/3 cup (25g) finely grated parmesan, plus shaved parmesan to serve
- Chopped flat-leaf parsley, to serve

METHOD
1. Heat the olive oil in a large deep frypan over medium-high heat. Add pancetta and cook for 3 minutes until crisp and lightly golden. Remove and drain on paper towel, then break into shards.
2. Carefully drain most of the fat from the saucepan, then return the pan to medium heat. Add the fennel seeds and cook, stirring, for 30 seconds or until fragrant. Add the butter and onion and cook for 7-8 minutes until onion is soft and lightly browned. Add the garlic, rosemary and thyme, then cook, stirring, for 1 minute.
3. Add the rice and cook for 2-3 minutes, stirring to coat the grains. Add the wine and simmer, stirring occasionally, until almost all the liquid has evaporated.
4. Add the hot stock, a ladleful at a time, stirring constantly and allowing each to be absorbed before adding the next, until almost all the stock is used and rice is creamy but al dente (about 20 minutes).
5. Add beans and parmesan to the risotto, then cook, stirring, for 1-2 minutes to warm through. Season with sea salt and freshly ground black pepper.
6. Divide the risotto among bowls and serve garnished with the crispy pancetta, a few thyme leaves, chopped parsley and shaved parmesan.

Blue-eye with a gluten-free herb crust

INGREDIENTS

4 slices gluten-free bread, crusts removed
2 tablespoons chopped basil leaves
2 teaspoons chopped thyme leaves
2 tablespoons grated parmesan
Grated zest of 1/2 lemon
1 eggwhite, lightly beaten
4 x 175g skinless blue-eye fillets
1 tablespoon extra virgin olive oil
3 cups (360g) frozen peas
2 cups mixed salad leaves

METHOD

1. Preheat the oven to 200°C. Line a baking tray with foil, then lightly grease.
2. Pulse the bread in a food processor to form rough crumbs. Add herbs, parmesan, lemon zest and eggwhite, season with salt and pepper, then pulse until just combined.
3. Brush the top of each fish fillet with a little oil and press some crumb mixture onto each fillet. Transfer to the tray. Bake for 10-12 minutes until the fish is cooked through and the topping is golden. Remove from the oven, cover loosely with foil and rest for 5 minutes.
4. Meanwhile, cook peas in a saucepan of lightly salted boiling water for 2-3 minutes until just tender, then drain.
5. Divide the peas and fish among plates and serve with salad leaves.

Lamb biryani (gluten-free)

INGREDIENTS

1 tablespoon sunflower oil
6 lamb fillets (500g total), cut in 2cm cubes
2 onions, thickly sliced
20 fresh curry leaves*
3 tablespoons (1/4 cup) gluten-free korma curry paste*
1 cup (200g) basmati rice
3 cups (750ml) gluten-free vegetable stock
2 tablespoons currants
Coriander leaves, to garnish
Mango chutney & gluten-free pappadams*, to serve

METHOD

1. Heat half the oil in a large heavy-based pan or casserole on high heat. Cook lamb for 3-4 minutes until just cooked. Transfer to a bowl.
2. Heat remaining oil over medium heat. Cook onion and curry leaves, stirring, for 3-4 minutes until onion is softened. Add paste and stir for 1 minute. Add rice, stirring to coat in paste, then add stock and currants. Bring to a boil, then simmer on low heat for 12-15 minutes, stirring often, until rice is tender.
3. Stir in lamb and heat for 2 minutes. Serve with coriander, chutney and pappadams, if desired.

Thai chicken cakes (gluten-free)

INGREDIENTS

4 small chicken breast fillets (about 600g total), roughly chopped
1 egg
1 1/2 tablespoons gluten-free Thai green curry paste
2 tablespoons fish sauce
2 teaspoons palm or caster sugar
Zest and juice of 1 lime
1/2 cup coriander leaves
4 kaffir lime leaves, finely shredded
2 tablespoons vegetable oil
Baby Asian salad leaves and sweet chilli sauce, to serve

METHOD

1. Place the chopped chicken in a food processor with the egg, curry paste, fish sauce, palm or caster sugar, lime zest and juice, and coriander leaves, then process until just combined. Transfer to a bowl and mix in the shredded kaffir lime leaves. Use wet hands to form the chicken mixture into 12 small cakes.
2. Heat the vegetable oil in a large non-stick frypan over medium heat.
3. Cook the chicken cakes, in batches, for 2-3 minutes each side or until golden brown and cooked through.
4. Serve the chicken cakes with Asian salad leaves and sweet chilli sauce.

Buckwheat noodles with spicy bolognaise (gluten-free)

INGREDIENTS

20ml (1 tablespoon) olive oil
1 onion, finely chopped
2 garlic cloves, crushed
300g pork mince
20ml (1 tablespoon) tamari sauce
1/2 teaspoon ground cinnamon
1/2 teaspoon dried chilli flakes
1 tablespoon mild paprika
150ml dry white wine or sherry
425g can crushed tomatoes
170ml can tomato juice
1/2 cup chopped coriander leaves, plus a few whole leaves, to serve
300g buckwheat noodles
1/2 telegraph cucumber, sliced

METHOD

1. Place oil in a saucepan over medium heat. Add onion and cook, stirring, until it softens. Add garlic and pork and cook, stirring, until meat has browned, breaking up any large lumps of meat with a fork. Add tamari sauce and spices and cook for 1 minute, then add wine and simmer for 2-3 minutes. Add tomatoes, tomato juice and seasoning.
2. Reduce heat to low and cook for 8-10 minutes until reduced and thickened. Stir in coriander.
3. Cook the noodles according to packet directions. Drain and divide between bowls. Top with bolognaise sauce and garnish with cucumber and the whole coriander leaves.

Baked Greek-style omelette (gluten-free)

INGREDIENTS

1/4 cup (50g) white long grain rice
1/3 cup (80ml) olive oil
3 leeks (white part only), thinly sliced
3 zucchini, coarsely grated
2 garlic cloves, crushed
1/4 cup chopped mint
2 tablespoons chopped dill
8 eggs, beaten
150g marinated feta cheese, drained, crumbled
Sliced red onion & tomato, to serve

METHOD

1. Preheat the oven to 180°C. Grease a 1-litre round ovenproof dish.
2. Cook rice in boiling, salted water for 8 minutes. Drain and refresh. Heat 2 tablespoons of oil in a saucepan, add leek and cook over low heat for 7-8 minutes or until softened.
3. Add zucchini and garlic, cook for 1-2 minutes, then add rice with mint, dill, eggs and feta. Season. Mix, then pour into dish and bake for 30 minutes or until golden and set.
4. Toss onion and tomato in remaining oil and place on top of omelette. Serve with a green salad.

Gluten-free coconut and cherry brownie slice

INGREDIENTS

250g unsalted butter, chopped
450g CADBURY Baking Dark Chocolate, chopped
6 eggs, lightly beaten
1/2 cup (70g) coconut sugar
1 1/2 cups (165g) coconut flour
1/2 cup (50g) Dutch cocoa powder
2 1/2 cups (310g) cherries, pitted, halved, plus extra cherries to serve
2 cups (180g) desiccated coconut
200ml pure (thin) cream

METHOD

1. Preheat the oven to 170°C. Grease and line a 20cm x 30cm lamington pan with baking paper.
2. Place butter and 250g chocolate in a heatproof bowl and set over a pan of simmering water (don't let bowl touch water), stirring until melted and smooth.
3. Remove from heat and quickly add eggs, sugar, flour, cocoa, 2 cups (250g) cherries and 1 cup (90g) coconut.
4. Stir until combined. Pour batter into prepared pan and gently tap on bench to remove any air bubbles. Bake for 25-30 minutes until the top has started to crack and a skewer inserted into the centre comes out with a few crumbs.
5. Cool in the pan for 20 minutes, then turn out onto a wire rack for a further 20 minutes to cool completely.
6. Meanwhile, place cream in a small saucepan over medium heat and bring to just below boiling point. Place remaining 200g chocolate in a heatproof bowl and pour over the hot cream, stirring until melted and smooth.
7. Set aside to cool for about 20-40 minutes until ganache is room temperature.
8. Place remaining 1/2 cup (60g) cherries and 1 cup (80g) coconut in a bowl, stirring until coconut is tinted pink. Remove the cherries and reserve for another use.
9. To serve, spread ganache over the brownie, scatter with pink coconut and top with the extra cherries.

Ice cream sandwiches

INGREDIENTS

1 cup (95g) quinoa flakes
1 1/2 cups (105g) shredded coconut, plus extra for rolling
2 cups (200g) almond meal
1/2 cup (70g) coconut sugar
2 tsp xanthan gum (from health food stores)
1/2 cup (100g) coconut oil
1/2 cup (175g) honey
2 tsp vanilla bean paste
1 tsp bicarbonate of soda
1L vanilla ice cream

METHOD

1. Preheat oven to 160°C. Grease 2 baking trays and line with baking paper.
2. Combine quinoa, shredded coconut, almond meal, coconut sugar, xanthan and a pinch of salt in a bowl. Set aside.
3. Place coconut oil, honey, vanilla, bicarb and 2 tbs water in a saucepan over medium-high heat and bring to a simmer. Remove from heat and pour over dry ingredients. Stir until a dough-like consistency. Divide dough into 12 balls, then roll into 8cm-wide rounds and place on prepared trays.
4. Bake for 12-14 minutes, swapping tray positions halfway, or until golden and firm to the touch. Set aside to cool completely.
5. Place small scoops of ice cream on a chilled baking tray lined with baking paper. With a piece of baking paper on top, flatten with your hand to the width of the biscuits. Sandwich each piece of ice cream with two biscuits, then roll edges in extra shredded coconut. Freeze for 30 minutes or until firm.
6. The sandwiches will keep in an airtight container in the freezer for up to 4 weeks.

Gluten-free Black Forest brownie

INGREDIENTS

270g unsalted butter, chopped
270g dark (70%) chocolate, chopped, plus extra finely grated to serve
6 eggs
1 1/2 cups (330g) caster sugar, 3/4 cup (75g) cocoa powder
75g fine corn (maize) flour (from health food stores)
3/4 cup (75g) almond meal
1 1/3 cups (200g) pitted fresh cherries

CHERRY SYRUP
1/2 cup (125ml) cherry juice (from grocers and delis)
1/2 cup (110g) caster sugar

MASCARPONE ICING
1/4 cup (60g) mascarpone
1/2 cup (60g) pure icing sugar
2/3 cup (165ml) pure (thin) cream

METHOD

1. Preheat oven to 150°C. Grease and line base and sides of a 20cm round cake pan with baking paper.
2. Melt the butter and chocolate in a heatproof bowl set over a saucepan of simmering water (don't let bowl touch water). Set aside.
3. Combine eggs and sugar in a separate heatproof bowl and place over the simmering water. Whisk for 8 minutes or until doubled in volume. Remove from heat.
4. Gradually whisk chocolate mixture into egg mixture until smooth. Gently fold through dry ingredients and cherries. Spread into the prepared pan.
5. Bake for 35 minutes or until a skewer inserted around the outer edge of the cake comes out clean and the centre is still slightly soft. Set aside in pan for 20 minutes, then transfer to a wire rack to cool.
6. For cherry syrup, combine juice, sugar and 1/4 cup (60ml) water in a saucepan over medium-high heat, stirring until sugar dissolves. Increase the heat to high, bring to the boil, then cook for 10 minutes or until thickened. Cool to room temperature, adding a little more warm water if too thick.
7. For the mascarpone icing, whisk all ingredients in a bowl to medium peaks.
8. Top brownie with icing. Drizzle with some cherry syrup and scatter with finely grated chocolate. Serve remaining cherry syrup on the side.

Sugar-free, gluten-free sticky date pudding

INGREDIENTS

½ cup honey
450g medjool dates, pitted
1 tsp bicarb
1 ½ tsp each mixed spice, ginger
2 cups almond meal
¼ cup coconut oil
1 tsb baking powder
3 eggs
Toasted almond flakes to serve

SALTED DATE CARAMEL

160g medjool dates, pitted
½ cup coconut cream
½ cup honey

METHOD

1. Preheat oven to 180.
2. Add the honey, medjool dates and 1 cup water to a saucepan and place over medium heat. Cook for 6-7 minutes then add bicarb, stir through and set aside to cool.
3. Meanwhile combine the remaining ingredients except the flaked almonds in a bowl and beat to combine.
4. Stir through the date mixture.
5. Grease and line a square 21cm cake pan.
6. Pour mixture into the pan then bake for 45 minutes. Remove and cool for 10 minutes.
7. Meanwhile for the date caramel, place all the ingredients in a blender and process until smooth.
8. Serve the sticky date topped with the date caramel and toasted almonds.

The low carb spaghetti

INGREDIENTS

1 butternut pumpkin, peeled, halved, seeds removed
1 bunch sage, leaves picked
2 garlic cloves, thinly sliced
4 slices prosciutto, torn into pieces
1/3 cup (55g) almonds, roughly chopped, plus extra to serve
60g grass-fed butter, roughly chopped

METHOD

1. Preheat oven to 250°C. Using a spiraliser, mandoline or vegetable peeler, turn the pumpkin into 'spaghetti'.
2. Spread over a roasting pan and top with sage leaves, garlic, prosciutto and almonds. Scatter butter over the tray.
3. Bake for 10-12 minutes until the butter is melted and a nut-brown colour and prosciutto is crisp.
4. Toss pumpkin to coat in butter and serve with extra chopped almonds.

Gluten-free chocolate banoffee tarts

INGREDIENTS

1 gold-strength gelatine leaf
200ml light thickened cream
200g dark chocolate (70%), roughly chopped
2 tsp vanilla extract
150g light cream cheese
1/2 cup (110g) coconut sugar, 200g silken tofu
2 x 400ml cans coconut milk, chilled overnight
2 bananas
Raw cacao powder (optional), to serve
1/3 cup (15g) flaked coconut, toasted, to serve

SWEET GLUTEN-FREE PASTRY

75g rice flour
1/2 cup (75g) chickpea flour (besan)
1/2 cup (50g) almond meal
2 tbs unrefined icing sugar
1 tsp xanthan gum
80g cold unsalted butter, chopped
1 egg

METHOD

1. For the pastry, place the flours, almond meal, icing sugar and xanthan gum in a food processor and whiz to combine. With the motor running, add the butter, piece by piece, until the mixture resembles breadcrumbs. Add egg and whiz until mixture comes together in a smooth ball. Enclose in plastic wrap and chill for 30 minutes.

2. Preheat the oven to 180°C. Grease eight 10cm loose-bottomed round tart pans.

3. Roll out the pastry on a lightly floured surface to 5mm thick, then use to line the pans, trimming any excess. Line with baking paper and fill with pastry weights or rice, then bake for 10 minutes. Remove weights and paper, then bake for a further 5 minutes or until golden and dry. Set aside to cool.

4. Meanwhile, soak the gelatine in cold water for 5 minutes. Fill a small saucepan one-third full with water and bring to a gentle simmer. Place the cream and chocolate in a heatproof bowl, place over the pan (do not let water touch the bowl) and stir until melted and smooth. Remove from the heat. Squeeze the excess water from the gelatine, then add to the chocolate mixture, whisking until gelatine dissolves.

5. Place the vanilla, cream cheese, sugar and tofu in a food processor and whiz until combined. Add the chocolate mixture and whiz until smooth. Divide the mixture among the tart cases, then chill for at least 2 hours or until set.

6. Spoon chilled coconut cream that has risen to the tops of the cans into a bowl (reserve the water for another use) and whisk to stiff peaks using electric beaters. Chill until ready to use (will keep for up to 2 days).

7. Peel and slice the bananas on an angle, arrange on top of the tarts and top with coconut cream. Dust tarts with cacao, if using, and sprinkle with toasted flaked coconut to serve.

Gluten-free carrot and galangal cake

INGREDIENTS

3 large carrots (about 400g), peeled, halved, cut into 3cm pieces
150g unsalted butter, chopped, softened
1/3 cup (75g) caster sugar
1/3 firmly packed cup (75g) dark brown sugar
1 tsp vanilla bean paste or extract
3 eggs
1 cup (120g) coconut flour
1 cup (200g) rice flour
2 1/2 tsp bicarbonate of soda
1 tsp each ground cinnamon and mixed spice
1/2 tsp freshly grated nutmeg
1/2 cup (85g) pitted dates, chopped
1/2 cup (70g) pecans, chopped
1 tbs finely grated galangal
1 tsp ground ginger
2 tbs icing sugar
Creme fraiche and maple syrup, to serve

METHOD

1. Preheat oven to 175°C. Grease and line a 1.5L loaf pan with baking paper. Place the carrot in a steamer set over a saucepan of simmering water. Steam for 40 minutes or until very soft, then mash to a chunky puree and set aside to cool completely.
2. Place butter, caster and brown sugars, and vanilla in a large bowl. Using an electric mixer, beat until thick and pale. Add the eggs, 1 at a time, beating well after each addition. Stir through carrot puree, then fold in remaining ingredients except ground ginger and icing sugar.
3. Pour into prepared pan and bake for 50-60 minutes until a skewer inserted into centre comes out clean. Cool cake completely in pan, then invert.
4. Dust cake with ground ginger and icing sugar. Slice and serve with creme fraiche and maple syrup.

Gluten-free pistachio amaretti morbidi

INGREDIENTS

1 1/3 cups (205g) pistachios, finely ground, plus slivered pistachios to serve
1/4 cup (35g) gluten-free plain flour, sifted
2 eggwhites, lightly beaten
1 tsp vanilla extract
1 cup (120g) pure icing sugar, sifted
100g dark chocolate, melted

METHOD

1. Preheat the oven to 180°C. Line two baking trays with baking paper.
2. Combine the ground pistachio, flour, eggwhites, vanilla and icing sugar in a large bowl, stirring until a thick paste forms. Roll 1 tbs dough into a ball, then place on trays and flatten slightly. Repeat with remaining dough, leaving a 4cm gap between each. Bake for 10 minutes or until cooked through.
3. Dip one half of each biscuit in melted chocolate, allowing excess to drip off, and place on a baking paper-lined baking tray. Sprinkle slivered pistachios over chocolate. Repeat with remaining biscuits, then chill for 15 minutes to firm up before serving.

Gluten-free fruit and nut loaves with sugar topping

INGREDIENTS

1 firmly packed cup (200g) brown sugar
250g natural yoghurt
3 eggs, separated
2 tablespoons vegetable oil
1 1/2 teaspoons gluten-free baking powder (see note)
1/2 teaspoon bicarbonate of soda
1 cup (125g) almond meal
1 cup (200g) rice flour
1 cup (140g) mixed dried fruit and nuts, roughly chopped

SUGARED TOPPING

50g white sugar cubes
1 eggwhite, whisked until frothy

METHOD

1. Preheat oven to 175°C. Grease and line base and 2 long sides of an 8-hole mini loaf pan with baking paper. Beat sugar, yoghurt, egg yolks and oil in a bowl with a wooden spoon until smooth. Stir in baking powder, soda, almond meal, rice flour, nut mix and a pinch of salt.
2. In a separate bowl, whisk eggwhites to firm peaks, then fold into batter. Spoon into holes almost to the top. Bake for 18-20 minutes until golden and risen.
3. For topping, place cubes in a zip-lock bag and crush with a rolling pin.
4. Brush tops with eggwhite. Sprinkle with sugar. Bake for 5-6 minutes until sugar slightly melts and a skewer inserted comes out clean. Cool for 20 minutes in pan. Lift out onto a wire rack to cool completely.

Gluten-free rose and pistachio cake

INGREDIENTS

230g salted butter, softened, plus extra for greasing
180g light muscovado sugar, 4 tsp rosewater
2 tsp vanilla extract, 4 large eggs, beaten
160g potato starch
3 tsp gluten free baking powder
160g ground almonds

FOR THE FILLING AND TOPPING

225ml double cream
1 quantity rose buttercream or extra whipped cream
50g pistachio nuts, finely chopped
Fresh or crystallised rose petals (optional)

METHOD

1. Preheat the oven to 180°C/Fan 160°C/Gas 4. Line the base of the cake tins with discs of baking parchment and butter the sides.
2. Cream the butter, sugar, rosewater and vanilla extract together in a bowl with an electric hand whisk or balloon whisk until light and fluffy. Gradually add the eggs, beating well between each addition. If it looks like the mixture is starting to curdle, add a couple of tablespoonfuls of the potato starch and beat again – it should come right.
3. Sift the potato starch, baking powder and ground almonds together over the mixture and fold in gently but thoroughly.
4. Scrape into the prepared tins and gently level the surface. Bake for 25–30 minutes until golden, springy to the touch and a skewer inserted into the centre comes out clean.
5. Leave in the tins for 10–15 minutes, then run a thin bladed knife around the inside of the tins. Turn out the cakes and place, right side up, on a wire rack. Leave to cool.
6. When the cakes are completely cold, whip the cream until thick, but not grainy. Put one of the cakes onto a plate and spread the cream almost to the edge. Place the other cake gently on top and twist it back and forth a little, just until the cream is peeking out between the layers.
7. Pipe or spread the buttercream over the top of the cake, or top with more whipped cream. Sprinkle with chopped pistachios and scatter over a few fresh or crystallised rose petals if you have them.

Gluten-free blueberry clafoutis

INGREDIENTS

3 cups (300g) almond meal
150g amaranth flour
1 tsp ground cinnamon
1 tsp nutmeg
2 tsp vanilla bean paste
200g honey
400ml extra virgin olive oil
4 eggs
300ml milk
250g blueberries, plus extra to serve
Sheep's milk yoghurt, to serve

METHOD

1. Preheat the oven 180°C. Grease a 20cm x 30cm x 5cm-deep ovenproof dish.
2. Combine the almond meal, amaranth flour, cinnamon, nutmeg, vanilla and honey in a bowl. Gradually add the oil and stir to combine. In a separate bowl, whisk the eggs and milk, then fold into the almond meal mixture.
3. Pour batter into the prepared dish and scatter over the blueberries. Set aside for 5 minutes to allow the berries to sink slightly into the batter.
4. Bake for 50 minutes or until slightly puffed and dark golden.
5. Serve clafoutis warm with yoghurt and extra blueberries.

Gluten-free coconut and lemon macarons

INGREDIENTS

2 eggwhites
2 1/4 cups (150g) shredded coconut
100g caster sugar
20g pistachios, chopped
Finely grated zest of 1 lemon

LEMON CURD

3 large egg yolks
1/4 cup (55g) caster sugar
1/4 cup (60ml) lemon juice, strained
100g cold unsalted butter, cut into pieces

METHOD

1. For the lemon curd, place the egg yolks and sugar in a heatproof bowl and whisk until thick and pale. Add lemon juice, then place bowl over a saucepan of gently simmering water (don't let the bowl touch water).
2. Cook, stirring with a spatula, for 2 minutes or until thick. Add cold butter, one piece at a time, and stir to combine, making sure each piece is incorporated before adding the next. Cook, stirring constantly, for 8 minutes or until curd is very thick and coats the back of a spoon.
3. Cool slightly. Cover surface with plastic wrap. Chill for 2 hours or until needed.
4. To make shells, preheat oven to 160°C. Line two baking trays with baking paper.

Poached peaches with low-fat ricotta and rose syrup

INGREDIENTS

1 cup (220g) caster sugar
4 peaches, halved
2 teaspoons rosewater
250g low-fat ricotta
2 tablespoons icing sugar
Edible dried rose petals* (optional)

METHOD

1. Place sugar in a saucepan with 2 cups water, stir over low heat to dissolve, then for 5 minutes. Stone peaches if easy; otherwise remove after poaching.
2. Add peaches to syrup and poach for 2-3 minutes each side (depending on ripeness) until soft. Remove, cool, then slip off skins. Add rosewater to syrup, cook 5 minutes until reduced and syrupy, then cool. Mix ricotta and icing sugar, place in a piping bag with a plain nozzle.
3. Fill peach halves with ricotta, drizzle with syrup and scatter with petals.

Gluten-free porridge with berries

INGREDIENTS

2 tbs tahini
2 tsp dark muscovado sugar, plus extra to serve
Greek yoghurt, mixed berries & mint leaves, to serve

GLUTEN-FREE PORRIDGE MIX

1 cup (140g) millet flakes (from health food shops)
1/2 cup (65g) amaranth flakes (from health food shops)
1/4 cup (25g) quinoa flakes
1 cup (70g) shredded coconut
100g macadamias, chopped
2 tbs each white chia seeds, flaxseed & sunflower seeds
1/2 tsp ground nutmeg

METHOD

1. Preheat oven to 180°C. Grease 2 baking trays and line with baking paper.
2. For the gluten-free porridge mix, combine all ingredients in a bowl and divide between prepared trays. Roast, stirring every 5 minutes, for 15 minutes or until toasted. Stand to cool, then transfer to an airtight container.
3. To make 2 servings of gluten-free porridge with berries, place 3/4 cup (110g) of porridge mixture, a pinch of salt flakes and 1 1/2 cups (375ml) water in a saucepan over medium heat and cook, stirring constantly, for 4 minutes or until mixture softens and thickens. Stir through tahini and sugar. Divide among serving bowls and top with yoghurt, berries, mint leaves and extra sugar.

Paleo cherry ripe

INGREDIENTS

2 1/2 cups (375g) dried cherries
100ml lemon juice
1/3 cup (115g) honey, plus 1 tbs extra
2/3 cup (165ml) coconut oil
1 cup (70g) shredded coconut
1 cup (100g) almond meal
3/4 cup (75g) cacao powder, plus extra to dust
1 cup (50g) coconut flakes, toasted
1/2 cup (70g) slivered almonds, toasted
1 tsp vanilla bean paste
30 fresh cherries, halved, pitted

METHOD

1. Place dried cherries, lemon juice, 1/3 cup (115g) honey and 1/3 cup (80ml) coconut oil in a saucepan over low heat, stirring, for 5 minutes or until softened and melted.
2. Transfer to a food processor with shredded coconut, almond meal and 1/4 cup (25g) cacao, then whiz until combined.
3. Transfer to a large bowl and stir through coconut flakes and slivered almonds.
4. Grease and line a 21cm square baking pan with baking paper and press mixture into the pan. Cover with plastic wrap and freeze for 2 hours.
5. Heat the vanilla, extra 1 tbs honey, remaining 1/3 cup (80ml) coconut oil and 1/2 cup (50g) cacao in a small saucepan over low heat, stirring until a smooth icing.
6. Slice into 15 bars using a hot knife. Dip bars in the icing and garnish with fresh cherry halves.
7. Set aside for 15 minutes, then dust with extra cacao to serve.

The gluten-free, dairy-free plum, lemon and olive oil cake

INGREDIENTS

2-3 plums, stones removed
2 large free-range eggs, at room temperature
70g (1/3 cup) unrefined icing sugar, plus extra to dust
1/2 teaspoon vanilla extract
2 teaspoons finely grated lemon zest
40ml extra-virgin olive oil
150g (1 /2 cups) almond meal
25g (2 tablespoons) fine brown rice flour
1/2 teaspoon gluten-free baking powder

METHOD

1. Preheat oven to 180C. Grease a 8-hole 1/3 cup (80ml) muffin tin and place two strips of baking paper crossing over each other in the base, extending up and over the sides by 2cm. Slice the plums into 1cm slices and place one into the base of each muffin tin.

2. Beat eggs, icing sugar, vanilla extract and a little pinch of fine sea salt using an electric mixer or handheld beater for 5 minutes, or until thick and pale. Add lemon zest and drizzle in olive oil, continuing to beat until just incorporated. Add almond meal and sieve over brown rice flour and baking powder, then gently fold in using a large metal spoon until just combined. Divide evenly between the prepared muffin tins and bake for 20-22 minutes or until a skewer comes out clean when inserted into the centre.

3. Remove from oven, cool in the tins 5 minutes before inverting onto a wire rack, remove paper strips and set aside to cool. Dust with icing sugar and serve slightly warm or at room temperature. Best eaten on the day of baking, however they will store for 3 days in an airtight container.

Gluten-free puddings

INGREDIENTS

500g mixed fresh summer berries (blueberries, strawberries, red-currants, blackcurrants, raspberries), plus extra raspberries, to serve
60g caster sugar
18 slices gluten-free bread
Yoghurt, to serve

METHOD

1. Place half the berries in a bowl, sprinkle with half the sugar and set aside.
2. Place remaining berries in a processor with remaining sugar and process until smooth. Sieve puree, discarding seeds.
3. Line four 200ml dariole moulds with plastic wrap. Using a small pastry cutter, cut out 4 circles of bread to line the base of each mould. Use a slightly larger cutter to cut out circles of bread for tops. Remove crusts from remaining bread and cut into 2cm strips.
4. Dip the bread bases in puree and place in base of moulds, then dip the bread strips and use to line sides of moulds. Next, fill the moulds with whole berries, packing well. Lastly, dip larger rounds in puree and place on top (chill leftover puree). Cover with plastic wrap, weigh down with a board and chill overnight.
5. Unmould onto serving plates, drizzle with leftover puree, top with berries and serve with yoghurt.

Pumpkin pie

INGREDIENTS

500g butternut pumpkin flesh, chopped
600ml coconut milk
2 cups (260g) pecans
6 dried dates
1 teaspoon pure vanilla extract
50g grass-fed butter, melted, cooled
1/4 cup (35g) coconut flour
3 eggs, 1 separated
2 teaspoons ground cinnamon
1 teaspoon ground nutmeg
1 teaspoon ground cloves
1 teaspoon ground ginger
Zest of 1/2 orange, finely grated
1/3 cup (80ml) maple syrup, plus extra to serve
1/4 cup (40g) pumpkin seeds (pepitas)
Coconut yoghurt, to serve

METHOD

1. Preheat the oven to 180C. Grease a 24cm loose-bottomed tart pan.
2. Place pumpkin and coconut milk in a pan over medium-low heat and simmer, stirring, for 25 minutes or until soft. Cool.
3. Meanwhile, whiz pecans and dates in a food processor until finely chopped, then combine in a bowl with vanilla, butter, coconut flour, 1 eggwhite and a pinch of salt. Press mixture into the base and sides of prepared pan. Prick base with a fork, then bake for 15-20 minutes until dry.
4. Whiz cool pumpkin mixture, spices, zest and 1/4 cup (60ml) maple syrup in a food processor. Add remaining 2 eggs and yolk, and whiz to combine. Pour filling into base. Bake for 45 minutes or until just set.
5. Toss pumpkin seeds in remaining 1 tablespoon maple syrup. Bake on a baking paper-lined baking tray for 8-10 minutes until golden. Cool, then break into shards.
6. Top pie with yoghurt, pumpkin seeds and extra maple syrup.

Gluten-free raspberry shortcake

INGREDIENTS

225g almond meal
3/4 cup (75g) skim milk powder
3/4 cup (60g) desiccated coconut
1/2 cup (100g) rice flour
2 teaspoons gluten-free baking powder
1 cup (250ml) gluten-free vanilla soy milk
500g low-fat ricotta
1 teaspoon vanilla extract
2 tablespoons icing sugar, sifted
3 punnets raspberries
1/2 cup (160g) low-joule raspberry jam, melted

METHOD

1. Preheat the oven to 170°C. Lightly grease a rectangular 10cm x 34cm loose-bottomed tart pan.
2. Combine the almond meal, skim milk powder, coconut, rice flour and baking powder in a bowl. Add the milk and stir to combine. Press into the tart pan and bake for 20-25 minutes until golden and cooked through. Cool completely in pan.
3. Process ricotta, vanilla and icing sugar in a food processor until smooth. Spread over the shortcake base, then cover with the raspberries. Just before serving, brush the berries with melted jam, then slice and serve.

Kelp noodles with poached chicken and miso

INGREDIENTS

1L (4 cups) chicken stock
1 bunch coriander, leaves picked, roots reserved
10cm piece ginger, halved
1 tbs fish sauce
4 x 200g skinless chicken breast fillets
2 tbs each white (shiro) miso paste, brown rice vinegar and mirin (all from Asian food stores)
1 tbs coconut oil
Juice of 1 lime
2 x 340g packets kelp noodles (we used Sea Tangle Kelp Noodles from Asian food stores), rinsed, drained
2 cups (100g) bean sprouts
2 long red chillies, thinly sliced on an angle
4 spring onions, thinly sliced on an angle
1 telegraph cucumber, halved, seeds removed, thinly sliced on an angle
4 sprigs Thai basil, leaves picked

METHOD

1. Bring the stock, coriander root, ginger, fish sauce and 1L (4 cups) water to the boil in a large saucepan. Add the chicken, remove pan from heat, then cover with a lid. Stand for 30 minutes or until chicken is white and cooked through.
2. Place miso, vinegar, mirin, coconut oil and 2 tbs poaching liquid in a saucepan over low heat and cook, stirring, for 4 minutes or until smooth. Remove from heat, stir in lime juice and cool slightly.
3. Remove chicken from pan, discarding liquid, and shred. Toss noodles, bean sprouts and half the chilli and dressing on a platter. Top with chicken, spring onion, cucumber, basil and coriander leaves, and remaining chilli. Drizzle with remaining dressing to serve.

Sesame-crusted salmon with sticky rice and bok choy

INGREDIENTS

- 1/2 teaspoon dried chilli flakes
- 4 tablespoons white sesame seeds
- 4 tablespoons black sesame seeds
- 1 tablespoon chopped flat-leaf parsley
- 1 eggwhite
- 4 x 150g salmon fillets, skinned, pin-boned
- 200g (1 cup) koshihikari rice
- 40ml (2 tablespoons) vegetable oil
- 1 1/2 teaspoons rice vinegar
- Steamed bok choy & tamari, to serve

METHOD

1. Combine chilli flakes, sesame seeds and parsley and spread on a sheet of baking paper. Place the eggwhite in a shallow bowl; lightly beat with a fork until frothy. Dip each salmon portion in the eggwhite, then cover with sesame mixture until each piece is well coated. Refrigerate for 10 minutes.
2. Place the rice in a pan with 1 1/2 cups water and bring to the boil, stirring occasionally. Reduce the heat to low-medium, cover with a lid and simmer for 15-20 minutes. Remove from heat and let stand, covered, for 5 minutes.
3. Meanwhile, heat the oil in a non-stick frypan over medium-high heat. Add the salmon pieces and cook for 3 minutes on each side. Add vinegar to the rice and stir to combine. Serve the salmon with sticky rice, steamed bok choy and a drizzle of tamari.

Pasta with chilli oil and grilled swordfish

INGREDIENTS
400g gluten-free pasta*
125ml (1/2 cup) olive oil, plus extra to brush
1 garlic clove, crushed
1 small red chilli, seeds removed, finely chopped
2 tablespoons sun-dried tomato paste
1 tablespoon flat-leaf parsley, finely chopped
4 (about 200g each) swordfish steaks
Lemon wedges, to serve

METHOD
1. Cook pasta in boiling, salted water according to packet instructions.
2. Meanwhile, place the oil, garlic and chilli in a saucepan over low heat for 5 minutes. Remove from heat and stir in the sun-dried tomato paste and parsley. Drain pasta and toss with chilli mixture.
3. Heat a chargrill pan until hot. Brush the fish with extra olive oil and cook for 2 minutes each side, leaving it a little rare in the centre. Divide pasta between plates, add a piece of fish and serve with the lemon wedges and a salad.

Thai beef salad (gluten-free)

INGREDIENTS

- 400g piece eye fillet
- 2 tablespoons crushed black peppercorns
- 1 teaspoon five-spice powder
- 1 tablespoon vegetable oil
- 100g rice vermicelli
- 1 tablespoon brown sugar
- 1/4 cup (60ml) lime juice
- 1/4 cup (60ml) fish sauce
- 1 long red chilli, seeds removed, cut into long strips
- 150g packet mixed Asian greens
- 2 Lebanese cucumbers, cut into batons Thai basil leaves and chopped peanuts, to garnish

METHOD

1. Preheat oven to 200°C.
2. Pat beef dry with paper towel. Combine peppercorns and five-spice and press onto beef. Heat oil in a frypan over high heat, then sear beef all over. Place on a baking tray in the oven for 6 minutes. Set aside to rest - the meat will be very rare.
3. Soak the vermicelli in boiling water for 2 minutes, then drain, refresh with cold water and drain again. Divide between 4 serving bowls.
4. In a separate bowl, combine the sugar, lime juice, fish sauce and chilli.
5. Wash and dry greens, then pile them onto noodles with cucumber. Thinly slice beef and place on greens. Drizzle with dressing. Top with basil and peanuts.

Pan-fried steak with rocket and blue cheese (gluten-free)

INGREDIENTS

2 red capsicum, roasted, cut into thin strips
1 cup mixed black and green olives
150g baby rocket leaves
2 tablespoons lemon juice
1/3 cup extra virgin olive oil, plus extra to brush
2 (about 150g each) porterhouse steaks
2 teaspoons chopped thyme leaves
1/2 cup (125ml) red wine
1 tablespoon balsamic vinegar
2 teaspoons brown sugar
120g mild blue cheese, crumbled

METHOD

1. Combine capsicum, olives and rocket in a bowl, then set aside.
2. Whisk together the lemon juice and olive oil until combined, season with salt and pepper, then set aside.
3. Heat a frypan over high heat. Brush steaks with extra oil, sprinkle with thyme and season with salt and pepper. Cook for 2 minutes each side, then rest for 5 minutes. Meanwhile, add the wine, balsamic and sugar to the pan and cook until reduced by half.
4. Toss rocket salad with oil and lemon dressing. Slice steak and place on the salad. Drizzle with reduced pan juices and scatter blue cheese over the top.

Lemon and garlic pork cutlets with lemon butter pilaf (gluten-free)

INGREDIENTS

4 (about 200g each) pork cutlets
1/3 cup (80ml) olive oil
1 garlic clove, crushed
1/4 cup (60ml) lemon juice
1 lemon, thickly sliced

LEMON BUTTER PILAF

1 tablespoon vegetable oil
20g unsalted butter
1 onion, finely chopped
2 cups (400g) white long grain rice
2 cups (500ml) chicken stock
1/4 cup (60ml) lemon juice
3 teaspoons finely grated lemon rind
1/3 cup finely chopped flat-leaf parsley

METHOD

1. Place pork in a bowl with 1 tablespoon of the oil, garlic, lemon juice and 2 teaspoons sea salt. Toss to coat, cover and refrigerate for 30 minutes.
2. Meanwhile, make pilaf. Heat oil and butter in a non-stick saucepan over medium heat, add onion and cook for 5 minutes until soft. Add rice, stirring to coat, then add stock and juice. Bring to boil, then reduce heat to very low, cover tightly and cook for 25 minutes (you can use a simmer mat to prevent rice from sticking). Fluff with a fork, add rind and parsley, season then cover to keep warm while you cook the pork.
3. Heat remaining olive oil in a nonstick frypan over medium-high heat.
4. Cook pork and lemon slices, in batches, for about 5 minutes each side or until the pork is golden brown and cooked as desired. Serve with the pilaf.

Paleo nachos

INGREDIENTS

2 large sweet potatoes, thinly sliced lengthways using a mandoline
1/3 cup (80ml) extra virgin olive oil
1 red onion, finely chopped
2 garlic cloves, chopped
1 red capsicum, finely chopped
1 small eggplant, finely chopped
350g lean beef mince
2 tsp ground cumin
1 tsp ground chilli
2 tsp dried oregano flakes
2 1/2 tsp smoked paprika (pimenton)
400g can chopped tomatoes
1 1/2 tsp Worcestershire sauce
1/2 cup (125ml) coconut cream, chilled
Juice of 1 lime
Charred jalapenos, halved avocado and coriander leaves, to serve

TOMATO SALSA

250g cherry tomatoes, halved
1/3 cup coriander leaves, roughly chopped
1 garlic clove, crushed
Juice of 2 limes

METHOD

1. Preheat the oven to 150°C. Place sweet potatoes in a single layer over 3 baking paper-lined baking trays and brush with 2 tbs oil. Bake for 15 minutes or until beginning to dry out. Reduce oven to 110°C and bake, turning and swapping trays every 15 minutes, for a further 1 hour or until crisp. Remove from oven and cool.
2. Combine salsa ingredients in a bowl, season with salt and set aside.
3. Heat 1 tbs oil in a large frypan over medium heat. Cook the onion, garlic and capsicum for 8 minutes or until softened. Remove onion mixture from pan and set aside. Add eggplant and remaining 1 tbs oil to pan. Increase heat to high and cook for 8 minutes or until tender and golden. Remove the eggplant from pan using a slotted spoon and set aside. Add mince, cumin, chilli, oregano and 2 tsp paprika to pan. Cook, stirring, for 5 minutes or until meat is browned. Add the tomato, Worcestershire sauce and 2 cups (500ml) water, then return onion, garlic, capsicum and eggplant to pan. Cook for 15 minutes or until thick and reduced. Season to taste.
4. Meanwhile, combine coconut cream, lime juice and remaining 1/2 tsp paprika in a bowl. Season with salt and set aside.
5. Arrange sweet potato chips in a serving dish and top with the spicy beef mixture, charred jalapenos, avocado, coriander, tomato salsa and coconut cream dressing.

Quick falafel with cucumber and herb salad

INGREDIENTS
800g canned chickpeas
1 tablespoon tahini paste*
1 cup flat-leaf parsley leaves
2 garlic cloves
1 teaspoon ground cumin
1 egg
Vegetable oil for deep-frying
Hummus, to serve

CUCUMBER & HERB SALAD
2 Lebanese cucumbers, halved, sliced
1/2 cup whole mint leaves
1/2 small red onion, thinly sliced
1 long red chilli, seeds removed, thinly sliced
1 tablespoon red wine vinegar
1 tablespoon olive oil

METHOD
1. Drain chickpeas, reserving 2 tablespoons of the liquid. Place chickpeas, reserved liquid, tahini, parsley, garlic, cumin and egg in a food processor and process until smooth. Season well with salt and pepper.
2. Form mixture into 8 flat patties. Half fill a deep-fryer or large heavy-based saucepan with oil and heat to 190°C (a cube of bread will turn golden in 30 seconds when oil is hot enough). Deep-fry falafel in two batches, for 2-3 minutes until browned. Drain on paper towel.
3. Place all salad ingredients in a bowl and toss to combine. Serve falafel with the salad and hummus.

Bacon-wrapped lamb cutlets with beans and fennel

INGREDIENTS
- 8 frenched lamb cutlets
- 2 teaspoons English mustard
- 4 rashers of streaky bacon, halved widthways
- 1/4 cup (60ml) olive oil
- 800g canned cannellini beans, rinsed, drained
- 2 small fennel bulbs, thinly sliced
- 2 tablespoons white wine vinegar
- 1/4 cup fresh parsley leaves

METHOD
1. Spread cutlets with mustard and wrap meat in bacon. Secure with a toothpick.
2. Heat 1 tablespoon oil in a large frypan over high heat. Cook cutlets (in batches) for about 3 minutes each side until bacon is crisp and lamb is medium rare.
3. Meanwhile, place beans and fennel in a pan with 2 tablespoons of water. Warm for 5 minutes over medium heat, then stir in vinegar, parsley and remaining oil.
4. Season and serve with lamb cutlets.

Baked ham on cranberry brown rice

INGREDIENTS

1 1/2 cups (300g) long grain brown rice
4 x 200g slices kassler pork* or ham steaks (1.5cm thick)
1 tablespoon olive oil
2 tablespoons maple syrup
1/2 cup (75g) dried cranberries*
1/4 cup roughly chopped mint
20g unsalted butter
1/2 cup toasted pecans, chopped
Steamed green beans, to serve
Wholegrain mustard, to serve

METHOD

1. Bring 3 cups (750ml) water to the boil in a large saucepan over medium-high heat. Add the rice, then lower heat to medium-low, cover and cook for 40 minutes or until tender.
2. Brush kassler or ham with oil. Heat a large, non-stick frypan over high heat and fry, in batches, for 1-2 minutes each side until lightly browned. Set the ham aside. Drain excess oil from pan and reduce heat to low. Add the maple syrup and warm through. Return meat to pan and coat with maple glaze.
3. Drain rice and place in a bowl. Add the cranberries, mint, butter and pecans and toss to combine.
4. Serve with ham, green beans and wholegrain mustard.

Chilli prawns with Brussels sprouts

INGREDIENTS

6 slices (80g) pancetta or bacon, cut into strips
600g brussels sprouts, trimmed (larger sprouts halved)
20g unsalted butter
1 tablespoon balsamic vinegar
1 tablespoon olive oil
2 garlic cloves, thinly sliced
1 long red chilli, deseeded, thinly sliced
20 green prawns (800g), peeled and butterflied, tails intact

METHOD

1. Preheat the oven to 200°C.
2. Place the pancetta strips on a baking tray and place in the oven for about 7 minutes or until lightly crisped.
3. Meanwhile, cook the brussels sprouts in a saucepan of boiling salted water for about 5 minutes until just tender, then drain. While still hot, place in a bowl with the crisped pancetta, butter and vinegar. Season with plenty of sea salt and black pepper, then toss to melt the butter and coat the sprouts.
4. Heat the olive oil in a large frypan over medium heat. Add the sliced garlic and chilli, and cook, stirring, for 1 minute until fragrant. Increase the heat to medium-high, add the prawns and cook, stirring, for 2-3 minutes until opaque. Divide the sprouts among bowls and top with the chilli prawns.

Barbecued mushrooms with feta

INGREDIENTS

300g fresh shiitake mushrooms, halved if large
200g swiss brown mushrooms, halved if large
300g oyster mushrooms, halved if large
1 tablespoon olive oil
2 garlic cloves, crushed
1/3 cup (80ml) balsamic vinegar
150g mixed salad leaves (such as frisee, mizuna and rocket)
1/2 cup flat-leaf parsley leaves
75g reduced-fat feta, crumbled

METHOD

1. Place the mushrooms in a bowl with the olive oil, garlic and 1/4 cup (60ml) of the balsamic vinegar, and toss to coat mushrooms in the mixture.
2. Heat a lightly oiled chargrill over high heat. When hot, add the mushrooms in batches and cook for 3-4 minutes, tossing occasionally, until cooked all over.
3. Place salad and parsley leaves in a bowl with the remaining tablespoon of balsamic vinegar, then toss to combine.
4. Divide the salad among plates, then top with mushrooms and feta.

Avocado and prawn risotto

INGREDIENTS

1.25L (5 cups) gluten-free vegetable stock
25g unsalted butter
1 tablespoon olive oil
1 onion, finely chopped
3 garlic cloves, crushed
2 cups (440g) arborio risotto rice
2/3 cup (165ml) dry white wine
500g green prawn meat, roughly chopped
1 cup (80g) grated parmesan, plus extra to serve
2 avocados
Juice of 1 lemon
1/4 cup roughly chopped chives

METHOD

1. Place the stock in a saucepan, bring to the boil, then reduce heat to low and keep stock at a simmer.

2. Meanwhile, heat the butter and olive oil in a deep frypan over medium heat, add the onion and cook, stirring, for 1-2 minutes until softened, but not coloured. Stir in the garlic, then add the rice and cook, stirring, for 1 minute to coat the grains. Add the wine and allow the liquid to evaporate. Add the stock, a ladleful at a time, stirring occasionally, allowing each ladleful to be absorbed before adding the next. Continue until you have one ladleful of stock left - this should take about 20 minutes. Add the prawns with the final ladleful of stock and continue to stir for 2-3 minutes until the prawns are cooked through. Stir in the parmesan, then cover and remove from the heat.

3. Peel the avocados, dice and toss in the lemon juice. Just before serving, carefully stir the avocado mixture into the risotto. Serve in bowls topped with extra parmesan and chopped chives.

Chicken with za'atar and tomato salad

INGREDIENTS

4 (about 180g each) chicken breasts on the bone
1/3 cup (80ml) olive oil
2 tablespoons za'atar*, plus extra to sprinkle
3 vine-ripened tomatoes, cut into wedges
1 cup flat-leaf parsley leaves
1/2 cup mint leaves
1 tablespoon white wine vinegar
Thick Greek yoghurt, to serve

METHOD

1. Preheat the oven to 190°C.
2. Place chicken breasts in a baking pan with 2 tablespoons of the oil and the za'atar. Rub the marinade onto the chicken, cover and and set aside in the fridge for 15 minutes.
3. Place chicken in the oven and cook for 25 minutes or until cooked through.
4. Place tomato and herbs in a bowl with vinegar and remaining oil. Season with salt and pepper and toss well.
5. Place chicken on serving plates, drizzle with pan juices, top with a dollop of yoghurt and sprinkle with a little extra zaatar. Serve with salad.

Poached salmon with raw vegetable salad

INGREDIENTS

1/3 cup (80ml) tamari
2/3 cup (160ml) mirin
1 garlic clove, crushed
1 teaspoon grated fresh ginger
4 salmon fillets, skinned, pin-boned
1 Lebanese cucumber, cut into thin batons
1 carrot, cut into thin batons
1 small yellow and 1 small red capsicum, seeds removed, cut into thin batons
6 radishes, cut into thin batons
Black sesame seeds, to garnish (optional)

METHOD

1. Place tamari, mirin, garlic, and ginger in a shallow fry pan, add 150ml water and bring to the boil. Lower heat and simmer gently for 2 minutes, then add salmon. Cover and cook for 3 minutes, then turn fillets and cook for a further 3 minutes.
2. Combine vegetables in a bowl. Place each piece of salmon in a serving bowl, top with vegetables and pour poaching liquid around. Garnish with sesame seeds.

Lamb stir-fry with coconut rice (gluten-free)

INGREDIENTS
2 tablespoons tamari*
1/4 teaspoon bicarbonate of soda
2 teaspoons arrowroot*
2 tablespoons sunflower oil
350g lamb backstrap, thinly sliced
3cm piece ginger, cut into thin strips
1 long red chilli, seeds removed, thinly sliced
1 carrot, peeled, cut into matchsticks
175g snow peas, ends trimmed, halved diagonally
Thinly sliced spring onions, to garnish

COCONUT RICE
200ml coconut cream
225g basmati rice

METHOD
1. To make rice, mix cream with 180ml water. Place rice and liquid in a large pan with 1 teaspoon salt and bring to boil. Reduce heat to low, simmer for 10 minutes, then drain.
2. Meanwhile, combine tamari, soda and arrowroot in a small bowl until smooth, then set aside. Heat half the oil in a wok over high heat and cook lamb in batches until browned. Remove and set aside.
3. Heat remaining oil and add ginger, chilli and carrot. Stir-fry for 1 minute, then return lamb to wok with snow peas and tamari mixture, and toss for a further minute. Serve with coconut rice and garnish with spring onions.

Risotto with chorizo, goat's cheese and peas

INGREDIENTS

- 1 tablespoon olive oil
- 200g chorizo, diced
- 20g unsalted butter
- 1 onion, finely chopped
- 1 small fennel bulb, finely chopped
- 1 clove garlic, crushed
- 350g arborio rice
- 1.2L gluten-free chicken stock
- 1 cup frozen peas
- 2 tablespoons chopped fresh mint
- 2 tablespoons grated parmesan, plus extra to sprinkle
- 150g goat's cheese, crumbled

METHOD

1. Heat olive oil in a large frypan over medium heat, add chorizo and fry until crisp. Remove chorizo and set aside.
2. Add butter to frypan, then cook onion for 1-2 minutes or until softened. Add fennel and garlic, cook for 1 minute further, then add rice. Cook, stirring, until all the grains are coated in the butter.
3. Gradually add stock, one cup at a time, stirring occasionally, until all liquid is absorbed. Add peas and cook for a further minute, then return chorizo to pan.
4. Just before serving, add the mint, parmesan and 100g of goat's cheese.
5. Divide risotto between 4 serving bowls and sprinkle with extra parmesan and the remaining goats' cheese.

Duck breast with raspberry vinegar

INGREDIENTS

4 duck breasts
90ml raspberry vinegar (available from gourmet food stores)
2 garlic cloves, crushed
1 tablespoon tomato paste
1 cup (250ml) red wine
2 tablespoons raspberry jam or redcurrant jelly
45g unsalted butter, chilled, chopped
150g baby salad leaves (mesclun)
Picked flat-leaf parsley sprigs, to garnish
150g fresh raspberries

METHOD

1. Score duck skin 3 or 4 times with a knife, then season. Heat a frypan over medium heat, place duck skin-side down and cook for 6 minutes until skin is crisp and fat has rendered. Turn over, reduce heat to medium-low and cook for 5 minutes. Remove, cover loosely with foil and set aside to rest.
2. Drain fat from pan. Return pan to high heat, add vinegar and reduce to about 1 tablespoon. Add garlic, tomato paste and wine and cook for 2-3 minutes until reduced by half. Add jam, cook for 1 minute, then whisk in butter a piece at a time. Season to taste.
3. Divide leaves between plates. Slice duck, then place on salad. Strain sauce over top. Garnish with parsley and scatter with raspberries.

Tomato and rosemary risotto cake

INGREDIENTS

350g arborio risotto rice
100ml olive oil
2 small onions, finely chopped
2 garlic cloves, crushed
3 zucchini, grated
3 eggs, beaten
1/3 cup (80ml) light thickened cream
3 tablespoons chopped rosemary
150g cherry tomatoes, halved
175g gruyere cheese, grated
Wild rocket and cherry tomato salad, to serve

METHOD

1. Preheat oven to 180°C.
2. Line the base of a 20cm non-stick springform cake pan with baking paper and grease well with butter.
3. Cook rice in boiling salted water for 10 minutes, then drain well.
4. Heat oil over medium heat in a heavy-based frypan. Cook onions and garlic until soft, add zucchini and cook, stirring, for 2-3 minutes. Cool, then add rice, eggs, cream, rosemary and tomato. Season, then stir in half the cheese.
5. Spread into cake pan and sprinkle with remaining cheese. Bake for 40 minutes. Cool slightly in the pan, then remove, slice into wedges and serve with salad.

Prawn and mango salad with spiced creme fraiche (gluten-free)

INGREDIENTS
50ml olive oil
Grated rind and juice of 1 large lime
1 tbs maple syrup
1/2 long red chilli, seeded, finely chopped
100ml creme fraiche or sour cream
4 cups baby salad leaves (mesclun)
1 mango, flesh thinly sliced
500g cooked prawns, peeled, tails intact

METHOD
1. For the dressing, whisk the oil with 2 tbs lime juice, then season.
2. In a small bowl, whisk together the remaining juice, rind, syrup, chilli and creme fraiche.
3. Toss salad leaves with dressing and divide among 4 bowls. Top with mango slices and prawns and serve with a dollop of spiced creme fraiche.

Pesto soup with zucchini and potato (gluten-free)

INGREDIENTS

- 1 tablespoon olive oil
- 1 leek (white part only), chopped
- 1 pontiac or desiree potato, peeled, chopped
- 1.25L (5 cups) gluten-free vegetable stock
- 2 zucchini, chopped
- 100g baby green beans, trimmed, cut into 2cm lengths
- 1 cup (120g) frozen peas
- 1/3 cup (80ml) gluten-free pesto
- Shaved parmesan, to serve

METHOD

1. Heat the olive oil in a large, heavy-based saucepan over medium heat, then add the leek and cook for 2-3 minutes until softened but not coloured. Add the potato and stock and bring to the boil, then reduce heat to medium and simmer for 5 minutes. Add the zucchini, beans and peas and cook for a further 2 minutes until potato is cooked and zucchini, beans and peas are just tender. Stir in the pesto and season. Ladle the soup into bowls and serve topped with shaved parmesan.

Best steak salad (gluten-free)

INGREDIENTS

650g chat potatoes, halved
1/4 cup (60ml) olive oil, plus extra for potatoes
2 garlic cloves, crushed
300g thick beef sirloin steak
300g thin green beans, trimmed, blanched, refreshed in cold water
1 small red onion, thinly sliced
100g cherry tomatoes, halved
2 tablespoons gluten-free mayonnaise
1 tablespoon red wine vinegar
1 tablespoon gluten-free horseradish cream
1 tablespoon chopped flat-leaf parsley leaves

METHOD

1. Preheat oven to 190°C. Toss potatoes with oil, salt and pepper on a baking tray and roast for 20-25 minutes until cooked.
2. Meanwhile, place 1 tablespoon oil in a dish with half the garlic. Season, then add steak and coat in the mixture. Set aside.
3. Place the green beans, red onion and halved cherry tomatoes in a bowl.
4. Mix mayonnaise, vinegar, horseradish, and remaining oil and garlic. Set aside.
5. Heat a chargrill over high heat. When hot, cook steak for 2-3 minutes each side, or until cooked to your liking. Set aside to rest for 5 minutes, then slice thinly and toss with salad ingredients and roast potatoes. Drizzle with the dressing, then sprinkle with parsley.

Veal saltimbocca

INGREDIENTS

4 x 130g veal escalopes (for schnitzel)
4 slices prosciutto, halved widthways
16 small sage leaves
2 tablespoons olive oil
40g unsalted butter
1 cup (250ml) white wine

METHOD

1. Place each veal escalope between plastic wrap and pound with a meat mallet until about 5mm thick. Halve each flattened veal piece widthways, then season meat.
2. Lay a piece of prosciutto on each veal piece and top with 2 sage leaves. Secure with a toothpick.
3. Heat oil and half the butter in a large, shallow frypan over high heat. When very hot, cook veal, prosciutto-side down, for 1 minute (in batches if necessary). Turn and continue cooking for a further 30 seconds, then transfer to a plate and keep warm. Pour wine into the pan to deglaze.
4. Bring to a boil and simmer over medium heat for 3-4 minutes until reduced, scraping up bits on the bottom of the pan.
5. Add the remaining butter and stir to melt.
6. Serve the veal with the sauce poured over, accompanied by baby green beans.

Coconut chia pudding with gluten-free spiced granola

INGREDIENTS

1 cup (250ml) coconut milk
1 cup (250ml) unsweetened almond milk
1/4 cup (40g) roughly chopped medjool dates
1 cinnamon quill
1/2 cup (80g) chia seeds
125g strawberries, roughly chopped

GLUTEN-FREE SPICED GRANOLA

2 cups (400g) quinoa, rinsed, drained
11/2 cups (210g) raw mixed nuts
1/4 cup (20g) desiccated coconut
2 tsp ground allspice
1/4 cup (70g) tahini
1/4 cup (90g) honey

METHOD

1. To make the chia pudding, combine the coconut milk, almond milk, date and cinnamon quill in a saucepan.
2. Place over medium-low heat, cover and bring to the boil. Remove from the heat and set aside to cool and infuse. Remove the cinnamon quill (rinse, dry and keep for future use).
3. Pour into a bowl and stir through the chia seeds. Cover and refrigerate overnight. For the granola, preheat the oven to 140°C and line a large baking tray with baking paper.
4. Combine the quinoa, nuts, coconut and allspice in a large bowl. Stir the tahini and honey together in a small bowl, then add to the quinoa mixture. Stir through until evenly combined. Spread evenly onto the tray and cook, stirring occasionally (be gentle as you want to it to clump into crunchy clusters), for 1 hour or until golden.
5. Cool completely and store in an airtight container for up to two weeks.
6. The next day, layer the chia pudding into bowls or jars with some granola and the strawberries.

Gluten-free caramelised carrot tart with carrot-top salsa verde

INGREDIENTS

Gluten-free plain flour, to dust
400g frozen Careme Gluten Free Sour Cream Shortcrust Pastry, thawed
1 bunch unpeeled mixed baby (Dutch) heirloom carrots
700g unpeeled carrots, cut into 3cm pieces
2 tbs extra virgin olive oil
1 1/4 tsp caraway seeds
4 eggs
1/2 cup (120g) sour cream
Labneh, dukkah and snow pea tendrils, to serve

CARROT TOP SALSA VERDE

1 garlic clove, finely chopped
1 tbs baby capers in vinegar, drained, finely chopped
1/4 cup (60ml) red wine vinegar
3/4 cup (180ml) extra virgin olive oil

METHOD

1. Grease a 18cm x 25cm fluted tart pan. Lightly dust a work surface with flour. Roll out pastry until 3mm thick, then use to line pan. Freeze for 1 hour.
2. Preheat oven to 200°C. Line pastry with baking paper and fill with pastry weights or rice. Bake for 25 minutes or until just dry. Remove the weights and paper, and bake for a further 10 minutes or until golden and dry. Set aside.
3. Meanwhile, reserve 2 baby carrots to garnish. Cut off tops from remaining baby carrots and wash and reserve, then chop flesh into 3cm pieces. Place in a microwave bowl with regular carrots, then cover with plastic wrap and microwave on high for 10 minutes or until slightly tender. (Alternatively, steam in a colander set over a saucepan of simmering water for 20 minutes.) Drain liquid, then place carrots on a baking tray. Drizzle with 2 tbs oil, scatter with caraway seeds and season. Roast for 40 minutes or until caramelised and tender. Cool. Reduce oven to 160°C.
4. Whiz the carrot mixture in a food processor to a puree, scraping side of bowl. Add the eggs and sour cream, and whiz to combine. Pour into pastry shell and bake for 40 minutes or until filling is set. Cool completely.
5. Meanwhile, for the salsa verde, finely chop reserved carrot tops, then combine with all remaining ingredients in a bowl and season.
6. Using a vegetable peeler, thinly slice reserved 2 baby carrots and place in a bowl of iced water. Drain just before serving.
7. To serve, spread tart with labneh and scatter with dukkah, snow pea tendrils, salsa verde and thinly shaved carrots.

Gluten-free zesty chicken and broccolini lasagne

INGREDIENTS

2 bunches broccolini
500g chicken mince
1 eschalot, finely chopped
2 garlic cloves, finely chopped
1 bunch oregano, leaves picked, 1/2 finely chopped
1 long red chilli, seeds removed, finely chopped
1/3 cup (80ml) extra virgin olive oil
2 cups (500ml) Massel Chicken Style Liquid Stock
1/4 cup (70g) tahini
400g can chickpeas, rinsed, drained
650g firm ricotta
1/2 cup (125ml) milk
2/3 cup (50g) finely grated parmesan
400g gluten-free dried lasagne sheets
1 tsp dried chilli flakes
2 tsp smoked paprika (pimenton)
Finely grated zest of 1 lemon

METHOD

1. Preheat oven to 180°C and grease a 2.5L (10-cup) ovenproof dish.
2. Place broccolini in a food processor and whiz until finely chopped. Set aside.
3. Combine mince, eschalot, garlic, chopped oregano, chilli, 2 tbs oil and 1 tsp each salt flakes and freshly cracked black pepper in a bowl.
4. Heat a large frypan over high heat and, in 2 batches, cook chicken mixture, stirring occasionally, for 3-4 minutes or until lightly browned. Return all chicken mixture to pan and add stock, tahini and 1/2 cup (135g) chickpeas.
5. Bring to the boil, then reduce temperature to a simmer and cook, stirring occasionally, for 5 minutes or until reduced slightly. Stir through broccolini and set aside to cool slightly.
6. Combine ricotta, milk and half the parmesan in a bowl.
7. To assemble lasagne, spread one-third of the chicken mixture into the prepared dish, then cover with a layer of lasagne sheets, breaking when necessary to fit. Spread 1/2 cup (120g) ricotta mixture on top, then cover with another layer of lasagne sheets. Repeat layering process two more times, finishing with remaining ricotta mixture.
8. Place a sheet of baking paper over lasagne, then enclose in foil. Bake for 40-45 minutes or until bubbling and cooked through. Remove foil and baking paper, and sprinkle with remaining parmesan. Increase oven to 250°C and cook, uncovered, for a further 20 minutes or until golden.
9. Meanwhile, place remaining chickpeas between paper towel and pat dry.
10. Heat remaining 2 tbs oil in a frypan over medium-low heat. Add chickpeas and chilli flakes, and cook, stirring occasionally, for 6-8 minutes or until golden and crispy. Stir through paprika and remaining oregano leaves. Spoon chickpea mixture over hot lasagne and scatter with lemon zest.

Gluten-free eggplant parmigiana lasagne

INGREDIENTS

- 3 x 400g eggplants, cut lengthways into 5mm-thick slices
- 100ml extra virgin olive oil
- 3 tsp dried oregano
- 2 cups (200g) almond meal
- 3 zucchini, thinly sliced lengthways
- 80g fior di latte cheese (from good delis – substitute mozzarella), coarsely grated
- 250g fresh buffalo mozzarella, torn
- 250g cherry truss tomatoes
- Store-bought pesto and basil leaves, to serve

CHUNKY TOMATO SAUCE

- 2 tbs extra virgin olive oil
- 2 garlic cloves, thinly sliced
- 4 anchovy fillets in oil, drained, finely chopped
- 1 tbs capers, rinsed, drained, chopped
- 650g roma tomatoes, chopped

METHOD

1. Preheat oven to 200°C. Grease 3 baking trays and line with baking paper.
2. Combine oil, oregano and 2 tsp salt flakes in a bowl and brush over eggplant. Arrange eggplant in single layers across prepared trays. Cover each tray of eggplant with a sheet of baking paper and roast for 40 minutes or until just cooked through. Remove from oven and set aside.
3. For the chunky tomato sauce, heat oil in a saucepan over medium heat. Add garlic, anchovy and capers, and cook, stirring, for 3-4 minutes or until garlic is light golden. Add tomato and 1 cup (250ml) water. Bring to the boil, then cover and reduce heat to medium-low. Cook for 20 minutes or until tomato has broken down slightly and sauce has reduced. Using a wooden spoon, stir to further break up tomato, then set aside to cool.
4. Place almond meal in a shallow dish. Brush eggplant slices with a little of the chunky tomato sauce, then gently dip in almond meal.
5. To assemble lasagne, grease a 35cm, 1.5L (6-cup) ovenproof dish. Spread half the remaining tomato sauce into the prepared dish, then cover with half the zucchini and eggplant. Cover zucchini and eggplant with the fior de latte cheese and spread over remaining tomato sauce. Top with remaining zucchini and eggplant.
6. Place a sheet of baking paper over lasagne, then enclose dish in foil. Bake for 45 minutes or until bubbling and tender when pierced with a knife. Increase oven to 220°C and remove foil and baking paper.
7. Top lasagne with mozzarella and cherry tomatoes, and return to the top shelf of the oven to bake, uncovered, for 20 minutes or until top is golden and tomatoes begin to blister.
8. Drizzle with pesto and scatter with basil leaves to serve.

Cold turkey salad with mango and honey dressing (gluten free)

INGREDIENTS

2 tablespoons seasoned rice vinegar
1 tablespoon caster sugar
1 garlic clove, crushed
1 small red chilli, seeds removed, finely chopped
500g leftover turkey (preferably breast meat), sliced
100g baby spinach leaves
2 cups mixed Asian herbs (such as coriander, mint, Thai basil)
1 large ripe mango, peeled, sliced
Black sesame seeds, to sprinkle

DRESSING

5 tablespoons (100ml) honey
1/4 cup (60ml) rice vinegar
100ml peanut oil
2 teaspoons sesame oil

METHOD

1. Mix together the rice vinegar, sugar, garlic and chilli, and stir until the sugar has dissolved. Pour over the sliced turkey and set aside.
2. To make the dressing, place the honey and vinegar in a food processor and process to combine. With the motor running, slowly add the peanut and sesame oils until a thickish dressing forms.
3. Place a pile of spinach on each plate and top with a handful of herbs, followed by some turkey. Lay slices of mango on top, drizzle with the dressing and sprinkle with the black sesame seeds

Tuna-stuffed capsicum (gluten-free)

INGREDIENTS

- 2 large red capsicum, halved, seeds and membrane removed
- 1 tablespoon olive oil
- 425g can tuna in oil, drained
- 2 hard-boiled eggs, chopped
- 1 tablespoon capers, chopped
- 2 tablespoons chopped chives
- 5 tablespoons (100ml) good-quality mayonnaise
- 200g wild rocket
- 1/3 cup (80ml) good-quality French dressing

METHOD

1. Preheat the oven to 180°C.
2. Place capsicum on a baking tray, cut-side up, drizzle with oil and roast for 15 minutes. Remove and cool.
3. To make filling, place tuna, egg, capers and half the chives in a bowl. Add enough mayonnaise to bind, and season with salt and pepper.
4. When capsicum are cool, fill cavities with the tuna mixture.
5. Toss salad leaves with half the dressing and place on serving plates with capsicum. Drizzle with remaining dressing, and garnish with remaining chives. Season with salt and pepper.

Tamarind and coconut fish curry

INGREDIENTS

- 2 tbs coconut oil
- 4 whole dried chillies
- 1 tbs brown mustard seeds
- ½ tbs coriander seeds, lightly crushed
- 2 sprigs fresh curry leaves, leaves picked, plus extra sprigs to serve
- 1 onion, thinly sliced
- 3 garlic cloves, crushed
- 1½ tsp ground turmeric
- ½ tbs tomato paste
- 400ml coconut milk
- 300ml fish or vegetable stock
- 1½ tbs tamarind puree
- 600g skinless chunky fish fillets (such as blue eye or ling), cut into 5cm pieces
- 150g cherry tomatoes, halved
- ¼ bunch coriander, leaves picked
- Steamed brown basmati rice and lime wedges, to serve

METHOD

1. Heat coconut oil in a large heavy-based saucepan over a medium-low heat, add dried chillies and mustard and coriander seeds, and cook for 1-2 minutes until fragrant and seeds start to pop. Add curry leaves, onion and garlic, then increase heat to medium and cook, stirring occasionally, for 5 minutes or until onions are soft.

2. Add turmeric and tomato paste and cook, stirring, for a further 2 minutes. Stir in coconut milk and stock, and bring to a simmer. Cook for 5 minutes or until sauce has thickened slightly and flavours have developed. Stir through tamarind, then add fish and simmer for 5 minutes or until fish is just cooked through. Stir through cherry tomato and coriander leaves (reserving a few sprigs to serve) to combine.

3. To serve, divide rice among serving bowls, spoon over curry, scatter with remaining curry leaves and reserved coriander sprigs, and serve with lime wedges.

Cavolo nero and 'nduja pizza

INGREDIENTS

1 1/2 tbs olive oil
2 garlic cloves, crushed
1 cup (240g) ricotta
3/4 cup (60g) finely grated pecorino
1/2 bunch cavolo nero, thick stalks trimmed, blanched, refreshed
80g 'nduja (Italian spreadable salami – from good grocers) or gluten-free spicy salami, finely chopped
1 long red chilli, halved lengthways
Sunflower sprouts and dried chilli flakes, to serve

PIZZA DOUGH

1 1/3 cups (200g) gluten-free plain flour, plus extra to dust
1/2 cup (75g) gluten-free self-raising flour
2 tbs flaxseed meal (from health food shops and selected supermarkets)
1/4 cup (35g) potato flour
1/4 cup (40g) gluten-free oat flour (from health food shops and selected supermarkets)
1 tsp (5g) dried yeast
1 tsp xanthan gum (from health food shops)
1 egg, plus 1 eggwhite, 1/3 cup (80ml) olive oil
1/2 tsp apple cider vinegar
1 cup (250ml) milk, warmed

METHOD

1. Grease a large baking tray and line with baking paper. For the pizza dough, sift the dry ingredients and 1 tsp salt flakes into a bowl.
2. Place the egg, eggwhite, oil, vinegar and milk in a stand mixer fitted with the hook attachment and beat until well combined. Gradually add the dry ingredients and beat until combined. Turn out dough onto a lightly floured work surface and knead for 2 minutes or until smooth. Transfer to a lightly oiled bowl, cover and set aside in a warm place for 45 minutes to rest (note: it won't rise like dough containing gluten).
3. Preheat oven to 200°C. Turn out dough onto a lightly floured work surface and roll into a large, 1cm-thick oval. Transfer to prepared tray.
4. To make the topping, combine 1 tbs oil, garlic and cheeses in a bowl and spread evenly over dough. Top with cavolo nero, 'nduja and chilli, and drizzle with remaining 2 tsp oil. Bake pizza for 20-30 minutes or until golden and cheese is bubbling (cover with foil if the top browns too quickly during cooking).
5. Scatter with sunflower sprouts, chilli flakes and salt flakes to serve.

www.ingramcontent.com/pod-product-compliance
Lightning Source LLC
Chambersburg PA
CBHW081417080526
44589CB00016B/2569